The
Effective
Writing
Teacher

The Effective Writing Teacher

EIGHTEEN STRATEGIES

by John Collins

Edited by Janet Angelis
Graphic design by Nick Thorkelson
Typesetting by Northeast Offset, Inc.

For Denise

Acknowledgements

To the many who reacted to the various drafts of this book: especially to Ruth Anne Shepard, Janet Angelis, Max McConkey and David Crandall of The NETWORK; to Aaron Stander of the Oakland Schools, Pontiac, Michigan; to John Meehan of the Pennsylvania Department of Education; and to the thousands of educators who have patiently listened to my ideas and provided me with suggestions and encouragement.

J.J.C.

Contents

Introduction

Most teachers have received little formal training in improving their own writing skills and even less in how to teach writing. *The Effective Writing Teacher* will help you better understand the *process* of writing — the steps a writer takes from generating ideas to producing a final product. It will also show you how to guide your students through that process to become better writers.

This method of teaching writing is, in fact, called the *process approach* by those who use it. Its most well known proponent is Donald Graves of the University of New Hampshire. It is the "new" way to teach writing and differs from the traditional, or product, approach in which teachers are likely to do little more than assign a composition and correct the final draft. Using the process approach, a teacher becomes involved in helping students progress through the various stages of the writing process.

There are a variety of ways to define the steps in the writing process, but the most common and simplest description of the process approach lists four stages or steps: prewriting, drafting, editing, and sharing. Throughout *The Effective*

Writing Teacher you'll find discussion organized around these four stages. Thus, the 18 strategies that form the heart of the book are divided into four chapters (Chapters II−V) called Prewriting, Drafting, Revision and Proofreading, and Sharing.

To help you decide which of the 18 strategies to select, I have included in Chapter I a brief Writing Program Assessment Survey that I often use in my workshops. Use it to evaluate your current writing program* and decide which strategies you need to adopt.

In addition, each of Chapters II−V begins with one or two strategies that are *preconditions* to a good writing program. Altogether there are six of these crucial strategies, and I call them the Critical Six. Whenever I ask teachers to take the Writing Program Assessment Survey, I find that the Critical Six receive the lowest scores, another reason that I have singled them out for attention. The Critical Six include:

Provide opportunities for students to discuss and clarify writing assignments before they begin writing.

Provide opportunities for students to get more information about a topic before they begin writing.

Provide specific information about the criteria you will use to correct each assignment.

Provide opportunities for students to review and revise written work completed earlier in the year.

Encourage students to edit each other's papers before they are handed in.

Provide opportunities for students to read written work out loud to individuals or to small groups of students.

*Readers should not be put off by my use of the term writing program throughout this book. If you engage in activities that help students become better writers, then you have a writing program — even if it is not formally sequenced or part of your written curriculum.

Because some of the strategies suggest doing things in different ways and because parents might have questions about your new methods, a copy of a letter you might send to parents is included in Chapter VI. It explains what you are doing and why and even offers suggestions for ways in which they can encourage their child to write.

Chapter VII offers a plan for effectively teaching writing using only five hours of class time per month. And Chapter VIII will help determine what skills you should be teaching your students.

The final two chapters (Chapters IX and X) offer some final advice as well as suggestions about where to look for further information on the subject of teaching writing effectively.

Writing is not easy to teach, but many teachers make it even more difficult by taking on themselves all the responsibility for producing a competent writer in one year. The attempt to develop too many competencies is almost as bad as doing too little, and the results are about the same — incompetent writers.

The Effective Writing Teacher will help you decide which skills you should teach and how to teach them effectively. The process described in this book is a process designed to eliminate wasted motion and help you focus on high impact activities. The result will be better student writers.

Chapter One

How Effective Is Your Current Writing Program?

The survey that follows will help you evaluate your current writing program. It will help you see where you're spending your writing instruction time, determine if you've been concentrating on the product or the process, and decide which steps to take first to make your teaching more effective.

Writing Program Assessment Survey

INSTRUCTIONS

For each activity (1-18), assign the rating that most accurately reflects how often you do the activity during the course of the year. If you are not sure how to respond to an item, make your best possible guess. Be careful not to overestimate; rather, try to think of actual times when you did the activities.

0 — Do not do this activity	3 — Regularly, once or twice a month
1 — Infrequently, a few times during the school year	4 — Frequently, three to six times a month
2 — Occasionally, less than ten times a year	5 — Very frequently, more than six times a month

I. Prewriting Activities   RATING

*1. Provide opportunities for students to discuss and clarify writing assignments before they begin writing. (Consider a writing assignment as any assignment that requires students to do more than one draft.) _____

*2. Provide opportunities for students to get more information about a topic before they begin writing (brainstorming, reading, discussing, interviewing, etc.). _____

3. Give writing assignments based on the personal experiences of the student. _____

II. Drafting Activities   RATING

*4. Provide specific information about the criteria I will use to evaluate each assignment. _____

5. Provide opportunities to write during class time. _____

6. Give writing assignments of a minimum of a paragraph in length. _____

7. Provide students with specific suggestions for improvement. _____

III. Revision and Proofreading Activities

*8. Provide opportunities for students to review and revise written work completed earlier in the year. _____

*9. Encourage students to edit each other's papers before they are handed in. _____

10. Teach grammar, usage, and mechanics in relationship to the students' current writing problems. _____

11. Teach editing skills (sentence combining, eliminating unnecessary words and phrases, checking for variety of language, organization, etc.). _____

12. Teach proofreading skills (punctuation, editing, symbols, manuscript form). _____

*One of the Critical Six

IV. Sharing Activities

*13. Provide opportunities for students to read their written work out loud to individuals or to small groups of students. _____

14. Give writing assignments that are meant to be read by readers other than myself. _____

15. Display or "publish" examples of high quality work. _____

16. Write along with students during class time, on the same writing assignment that they are working on. _____

17. Write positive comments on students' work. _____

18. Conduct individual writing conferences with students. _____

Scoring

First look at the pattern of your scores. Do you have all 2s or all 5s or are the scores evenly dispersed? Clearly, the closer the scores come to the 4 or 5 end of the scale, the better. A question often asked is, "What is the lowest possible total score a teacher could have and still have an effective wrting program?" This question is impossible to answer exactly because the time available for writing, the abilities and grade levels of the students, and classroom resources all have a

*One of the Critical Six

significant influence on what a teacher can do. Nevertheless, a total score within the range of 54 to 72 is acceptable. The closer the score is to 90, the better.

A score lower than 54 (18 items multiplied by an average score of 3, monthly) indicates that there is not enough consistent application of the activities over time. Activities done randomly do not make an effective writing program.

When you've examined the scores in a general way, look at the scores for each of the four sections of the survey: prewriting, drafting, editing, and sharing. Does one section seem disproportionately low or high? Does your program have high scores on the editing section and low scores on the sharing section?

Of course many of the activities are beneficial and appropriate at more than one step in the process. For example, I consider item 13 (Provide opportunities for students to read their written work out loud) as the single most important activity under two categories: sharing and drafting. Its value as a sharing activity is obvious, but as a drafting activity it has equal value because it makes the writer listen to the message rather than focus on each individual word. Additional examples of activities that have an impact on more than one phase of the writing process include items 9 (peer editing) and 4 (provide information on grading criteria). Both of these activities help in the drafting *and* revision phases. Therefore, consider the grouping as a way of demonstrating that the activities cover all the elements of the process approach and realize that many activities can bring improvement at more than one stage.

Now examine your scores for items 1, 2, 4, 8, 9, and 13 — the Critical Six. Scores of 3, 4, or 5 on these activities almost ensure that your program is headed in the right direction.

After you've examined the results, select two activities that you feel could strengthen your program the most. You might choose your two lowest scores or two strategies from the section with the lowest scores. They could be two of the Critical Six or activities from one of the steps in the writing process that you feel could benefit your students most. Or you might want to read more about the writing process and the 18 strategies (Chapters II-V) before you decide where to begin.

The rest of this book is designed to provide help implementing whatever strategies you select. Following the discussion of each of the 18 strategies and the suggestions on how to implement them, you'll find a plan for putting them all together (Chapters VI-VIII).

Chapter Two

Prewriting Activities

STRATEGIES 1 – 3

Prewriting activities are simply the things a person should do before she or he begins to write — the thinking, talking, or information gathering one needs to do to know enough to have something to say.

While it is not true that students have to know what they're going to write before they put pencil in hand, it is necessary that they have a clear notion of the assigned topic. It will also be easier for them to write if their heads are full of ideas. The activities in this chapter are designed to help you clarify assignments and generate ideas to give students a good start.

STRATEGY 1

Provide opportunities for students to discuss and clarify writing assignments before they begin writing.

This is one of the Critical Six activities. It is especially important as you begin to give students assignments that have a specific purpose (e.g. describe a place you know well in such a way that your reader will want to visit it). In primary grades, where much of the writing is narrative and descriptive and based on personal experience, students need less help in clarifying the assignment. But if you have a specific purpose or audience in mind when giving an assignment, then be sure to include enough time to explain both.

During discussion time the students can clarify the purpose and audience for themselves and/or negotiate with you to modify the assignment so they will find it more interesting. The clearer your intent and the more interesting the assignment, the shorter and simpler this activity will be. If you are confused about what it is you wish the students to accomplish by completing a particular writing assignment, you will discourage their creativity and drive them to write simply to get it over with.

As a general rule, if you give a specific writing assignment — as opposed to letting students select their own topic and approach — you should try to structure the assignment so that it has the following elements:

- **purpose** — something that makes the assignment more than just an activity to get a grade (for ideas, see the examples that follow);
- **audience** — someone the writer should be writing to — someone other than the teacher, if possible; and
- **form** — a statement about how the composition should be structured, for example, as a letter or advertising copy or a memo.

For instance, a typical writing task, a book report, can be turned into a variety of writing assignments that have more value and interest than a simple descriptive summary of a book. Students can create book jacket copy to motivate other students to read the book, or write a letter to the author giving their reactions to the book, or write a critical review so that other students can get a sense of the book's strengths and weaknesses. Such assignments are better than the standard book report because they have a purpose, specify an audience, and suggest a form or format.

One of my favorite writing assignments comes from a middle school social studies teacher who requires that students write a letter to an imaginary pen pal in England after each of nine units in American history. Specifically, the assignment places the student in the historical period that was just covered. Students must describe some of the major historical events and some of the realities of day-to-day living during that period. Students date the letter to reflect the time period they are "living in" and use standard letter form. While the letters are never mailed, students look forward to reading one another's, and the teacher claims that the brainstorming session he conducts (see Strategy 2) generates more good questions on the historical period than any other activity.

When students write these letters, they discover how much they know. They also discover what it is they don't know and need to find out.

STRATEGY 2

Provide opportunities for students to get more information about a topic before they begin writing.

Another of the Critical Six activities is brainstorming. After you've clarified the assignment (Strategy 1), spend time talking about the assignment before students begin writing. Don't worry about students stealing one another's ideas. Rather, fill the air with ideas! Try to generate more ideas than any one writer could use.

Remember, the brainstorming process is a very specific one. It involves setting a *high quota* for the number of ideas that must be generated and specifying a *time limit* during which the quota must be reached. *Negative comments are not permitted* — no matter how bizarre or inappropriate the brainstormed ideas may seem. Also, remember that experts in creativity suggest a warm-up brainstorming activity about something unrelated to the topic (e.g., how many ways can you use worms or broccoli) before students begin to brainstorm about a more serious topic. Usually it's best if you act as the recorder, using the blackboard, an easel pad, or butcher paper.

In my teaching experience, especially in the lower and middle grades, I have found that asking students to both take notes and to brainstorm was asking too much. Their note-taking slowed down their idea-generating and the session lost its spontaneity and excitement. Therefore it's best to ask your students to clear their desks and concentrate on adding to the ideas you record.

After you and the class have gotten comfortable with the general mechanics involved in generating and recording brainstorms, you might want to try some refinements. One alternative process involves using a student recorder in addition to yourself. Select one student, someone who has good penmanship and spelling skills, and give that student a ditto master. Have the students brainstorm on a topic while you record their ideas on the board. The student recorder copies the ideas onto the ditto master. At the end of the brainstorming session, the recorder can give you the ditto master with the notes copied from the board, so that you can reproduce and distribute them at the end of class or at the end of the day.

Also, once you and/or your students get good at recording, you might try a three-column system: one column for general ideas, one column for specific suggestions about the ideas, and one for vocabulary words or phrases that students might find helpful. This scheme works for most brainstorming topics and yields an end product that's really useful as students enter the drafting stage of the writing process.

Brainstorming is important as a way of generating ideas and getting students started, but do not let students push you to continue the brainstorming/discussion phase indefinitely. "You must have something to say in order to write," is a myth. Writing will help writers discover ideas and opinions that they did not know they had. Authors continually state that they must write to discover what they know. "Thought comes with writing, and writing may never come if it is postponed until we are satisfied that we have something to say" (Smith 1981).

STRATEGY 3

Give writing assignments based on the personal experiences of the student.

For many students, at all grade levels, writing is difficult enough without having to invent ideas to write about. For young children, the opposite is sometimes true because they are so good at using fantasy, but in general, personal experience is the richest place for good writing to begin.

An additional advantage to writing about personal experience, thoughts, or ideas is that it forces the writer to be reflective and to draw meaning out of his or her experience. Insisting that students draw conclusions about their experience will help them move beyond writing anecdotes. Many educators consider reflecting on past experience the essence of education.

Ask students to keep a list of "Topics I Would Like to Write About" in their writing folders*. Periodically give students a chance to review and add to this list.

Students at all grade levels need a balance between compositions on teacher assigned topics and compositions that require them to develop and refine a topic. In general, the

*Here and throughout the book, I refer to writing folders. I have found the writing folder an invaluable tool in an effective writing program. I have created one such tool, the Cumulative Writing Folder.™ The folder is available in packages of 25, complete with directions and tips for the teacher, and can be ordered from The NETWORK, Inc., 300 Brickstone Square, Suite 900, Andover, Mass. 01810.

weaker the students' writing skills, the more the assignments need to be freely chosen, so that they can build their confidence through experiencing success.

As students become more skilled writers, the balance between writing about personal experience and writing about more limited and academic topics begins to shift, and more assignments can be teacher directed. For high school students who intend to go on to college, writing instruction becomes vocational education. College bound students need to learn to develop a topic they have *not* selected and apply information they have or acquire through research to support a thesis. This type of expository writing is the type required in most essay examinations and should be taught when the student has acquired a command of basic writing skills.

Chapter Three

Drafting Activities

STRATEGIES 4 — 7

Once prewriting discussions have clarified a writing assignment, students should be able to draft — commit their thoughts to paper. If they also know what criteria you'll be using when you correct, the drafting task will be easier. That's why the first strategy in this chapter deals at length with the Focus Correction System. Only after students actually begin to write do difficulties with an assignment become apparent. It is important to provide some class time for drafting so students can ask questions at this point. And, as often as time permits, try completing your own assignment and write alongside your students.

STRATEGY 4

Provide specific information about the criteria you will use to evaluate each assignment.

This is the third of the Critical Six strategies. Providing specific information about the criteria you will use to correct each assignment is called *focus correcting*. Focus correcting is a selective approach to correcting student writing. It takes place when a teacher selects one, two, or three areas that are critical problem areas and corrects for *only* those areas. You may select any area for focus correcting, from word choice to interesting beginning sentences.

The focus correction areas can be selected for an individual, a group, or a total class. Using the Focus Correction System requires a great deal of self-discipline on the part of the teacher, but the time saved and the rewards gained are well worth the initial effort.

The advantages of focus correcting are supported by considerable research. Recently over 500 experimental studies on the effectiveness of certain types of writing instruction were examined.

> Scales, criteria, and specific questions which students apply to their own or others' writing also have a powerful effect on enhancing quality. Through using the criteria systematically, students appear to internalize them and bring them to bear in generating new materials even when they did not have the criteria in front of them (Hillocks 1984).

When using focus correcting, teach the skill the student needs when the assignment is initially given or at least *before* the paper is in final draft form. If students know that the compositions are being corrected for only a few critical areas, and if they know how to fix the problems in these areas, then they can also edit each other's work (see Strategy 9).

To realize the full benefits of focus correcting, you must avoid the temptation to overcorrect. When correcting compositions, indicate problems only in the selected focus correction area(s). Build up to two or three focus correction areas per composition, but do not drop an area until you see substantial progress.

Implementing focus correcting is the most difficult activity of the Critical Six. It runs contrary to most of our experiences as students — when our papers were corrected for every error in every line — and as teachers. But think about the reality in your classroom: how often do you see a student carefully examining a corrected paper, looking at each error?

Most students want to know the grade and be done with it. Focus correcting changes this by saving correcting time and helping the student consider the quality of the paper in relationship to a few clearly specified criteria rather than an infinite number of highly subjective criteria.

When assigning focus correction areas mix stylistic and mechanical areas. *Do not limit focus correcting to simply correcting mechanical errors* such as capitalization and punctuation. If you do so, students will soon feel that good writing means trying to avoid punctuation and spelling errors. If students develop this attitude, their desire to write well will be destroyed. Remember, encouraging students to write a beginning that will make the reader want to read on is as important as encouraging students to avoid run-on sentences.

The lists of focus correction areas shown below are not intended to be all-inclusive. They provide examples of 24 important correction areas and include areas that are both stylistic and mechanical.

EXAMPLES OF FOCUS CORRECTION AREAS FOR STYLE

1. Is the composition easy to read out loud? Does it flow naturally?
2. Can the writer eliminate any unnecessary words?
3. Does the composition have a strong, clear ending?
4. Does the writer use sensory details?
5. Are the sentences too long? Are they confusing?
6. Are the sentences too short? Are they monotonous?
7. Is there a balance between long and short sentences, between simple and complex sentences?
8. Does the writer use transitions between sentences?
9. Does the writer use transitions between paragraphs?
10. Is the topic too general? Too trivial?
11. Does the beginning try to capture the reader's interest?
12. Does the writer avoid cliches or overused words?
13. Does the writer use specific details to support general statements?
14. Does the writer use similes and metaphors?
15. Can the writer make the composition more interesting by answering the question when or why or where or how?
16. Is the topic appropriate for the audience?
17. Does the conclusion reinforce the focus of the composition?
18. Are the ideas developed in proportion to their significance?

EXAMPLES OF FOCUS CORRECTION AREAS FOR MECHANICS

1. Is the penmanship legible and the prose well laid out?
2. Is the final draft in the correct form?
3. Does the writer correctly use quotation marks?
4. Does the writer underline the names of books and plays, etc.?
5. Are there too many sentences in each paragraph?
6. Does the writer correctly use a semicolon or a comma with coordinating conjunctions to punctuate sentences?

Outlined below is *one way* the Focus Correction System can be introduced and maintained in a classroom at any grade level. The three-step process will help you select the first set of focus correction areas. This system applies only to the first assignment you give.

Step One: Give your students a short writing assignment to do in class. Select a general topic for the assignment and have a ten to fifteen minute discussion about the topic to generate ideas for those students who might be experiencing "writer's block."

Provide enough time so that even your slower writers will be able to complete the assignment without undue haste. If dictionaries are available, encourage your students to use them. Collect the first drafts.

Step Two: Do not review the papers, but return them to the students in a subsequent class, encouraging them to improve their compositions in any way they can. Some students can improve their writing by being given an opportunity to take a fresh look at their compositions with time to make improvements. Collect the second drafts of the compositions.

Step Three: Read papers over without grading them. For each paper identify the two or three major problem areas. These might be minor errors that occur frequently, or more important errors that occur less often, or both. The areas you choose will depend upon your writing program and the level you teach. From this list select only four or five focus correction areas that will be your emphasis for the year. Do not try to do 20 in a year. Teach your students to master a few writing skills rather than merely expose them to many skills. Believe me, if you can eliminate three or four of the major writing problems of students in your class, then it will be a good year!

One way to avoid being overwhelmed by the number of errors you find in the writing samples is to simply put papers into one of three piles: 1) compositions that say too much or are too long, 2) compositions that are well developed and are of adequate length, or 3) compositions that do not say enough.

Divide your students into three groups that correspond to the three piles. Work with the students who have not written enough by teaching them how to expand their text; for example, have students answer the questions who, what, why, etc. Next, work with the students who don't know how to limit their compositions by teaching them organizing skills; for example, "Give the *two* strongest reasons for your opinion."

With students in the second group — those who write enough — move to activities that have them examine word choice, develop a more interesting beginning, use more specific supporting details, or write on a more daring idea. This last group of students can also be assigned fewer but longer compositions.

See Chapter VIII, "What Writing Skills Should Be Taught," for additional information on selecting focus correction areas.

STRATEGY 5

Provide opportunities to write during class time.

By writing I mean putting thoughts down on paper with concern about the ideas *and* the presentation of these ideas. Fill-in-the-blank or one-sentence answers cannot be considered writing. Multi-sentence answers that require students to attend to the correctness of the answer and the correctness of the presentation of the answer is writing. The best writing assignments require that students define the general area, select from a wide variety of information or experience about the area, and present information with a specific audience, purpose, and format in mind. Most writing in response to test items does not meet these criteria.

Finding time for students to write during class time is less a problem in the elementary grades than in junior or senior high school. In *Writing in the Secondary School*, Arthur Applebee reports the results of his investigations about the amount of time students spend writing in high schools:

> Using a broad definition of writing, an average of 44 percent of the observed lesson time involved writing activities, with mechanical uses of writing (such as short-answer and fill-in-the-blank tasks) occurring 24 percent of the observed time, note-taking 17 percent, and writing of paragraph length or longer occurring 3 percent of the observed time. Similarly, homework assignments involved writing of at least paragraph length 3 percent of the time (1981).

Class time spent in writing can be the most valuable at the beginning and the end of the writing process. Students should be given time to organize their drafts and to write the first few lines while the teacher is available to help clarify the assignment. You can also provide encouragement to students to experiment and to consider many ideas and approaches.

Students need class time during the editing stages to use peers for reactions and proofreading and, if necessary, to ask the teacher for technical advice. Learning how to organize and begin a composition and learning how to polish it into final form are the two most troublesome areas for writers at all levels. If you can provide class time and advice at these stages, the in-class time will be easily justified in relationship to the improved student skills that will result.

STRATEGY 6

Give writing assignments of a minimum of a paragraph in length.

The paragraph, not the sentence, is the best unit of instruction for writing. Encourage your students to write paragraphs. Indeed, the majority of your writing assignments should be short — a paragraph in the lower grades, a few paragraphs in the upper grades. In the lower grades, students need practice composing paragraphs with supporting details. In the upper grades, students need to learn how to express their ideas with brevity and clarity.

Don't confuse quantity with quality. Most students simply do not know how to draft or proofread. Long writing assignments encourage students to fill pages to please the teacher and take away from the energy they have to practice editing and refining. On the other hand, writing assignments that require only short fill-in-the-blank type answers or single sentences will not teach students how to organize and develop ideas. Try to strike a happy medium.

STRATEGY 7

Provide students with specific suggestions for improvement.

Many teachers indicate student errors but do not explain how to fix these errors. I believe it is better writing instruction to indicate all the errors in one area and suggest ways to correct these errors. In the columns below, I have listed typical teacher comments that I see all the time on papers and helpful teacher comments that I rarely see on papers.

TYPICAL TEACHER COMMENTS	HELPFUL TEACHER COMMENTS
1. Avoid punctuation mistakes.	You have a problem with contractions. See the grammar book, pages 101 and 102, and do the lesson. If you need an explanation, ask me or another student.
2. Too many run-on sentences.	Watch for sentences longer than twenty words. I've indicated where you've made run-on sentence errors.

TYPICAL TEACHER COMMENTS	HELPFUL TEACHER COMMENTS
3. Improve usage.	You seem to be confused about when to use *to*, *two*, and *too*. Read page 75 in the grammar book and correct your paper. I've corrected the first few errors to get you started.
4. Awkward sentences.	Please read this paper over, out loud. After you have read it out loud have another student read it out loud to you. Listen for the places where you have to read very slowly. Rewrite those sections so that they can be read smoothly.

No doubt you noticed that the helpful teacher comments are much longer than the typical teacher comments; therefore, try to limit the number of corrections and the number of suggestions for improvement. See Strategy 4 (Provide specific information about the criteria you will use to evaluate each assignment) in this chapter for a description of focus correcting and how to implement this technique.

You will find focus correcting will save you a great deal of time, and students will find that it puts them in the position of being able to make improvements on their papers without being overwhelmed by the number of errors and by the challenge of having to determine how to correct many different types of errors.

Chapter Four

Revision and Proofreading Activities

STRATEGIES 8 – 12

Teaching editing is the most complicated step in the writing process because it involves teaching students to first review their work by looking at the forest — the overall design, flow, organization — and then to examine the trees — the sentences, punctuation, spelling. This chapter suggests several strategies for teaching students to take the time to become good editors.

STRATEGY 8

Provide opportunities for students to review and revise written work completed earlier in the year.

You cannot have an effective writing program unless you require students to save their final drafts in some sort of a writing folder. Students must be able to review past work, see progress, and note where more work is still needed. In addition, any student who writes 15 to 25 compositions a year deserves to have his or her teacher design a system to keep these compositions. Mary Smith needs to feel the joy of having the "Collected Works of Mary Smith." One of the Critical Six activities is to have students review and revise the work in these folders.

Teachers — as well as students — need to be able to look back and see change and progress. Writing is one of the few areas of teaching that, if done effectively for a year, may still produce students who make more errors in June than in September. For example, if you have done an excellent job, many students will write longer, more detailed compositions, with varied sentences and richer vocabulary. Your students will take more risks. All of these extremely positive behaviors might lead to more errors, but they will be "more sophisticated" errors. Unless you can compare September's paper — with the short sentences and basic vocabulary — to June's, you will not be able to see progress and will end up feeling like, "The faster I go, the behinder I get."

But the most compelling reason for students to collect compositions is that they provide the best source of editing practice. For example, you would like to begin a series of lessons on writing interesting beginnings. Traditionally, you might have begun by using the activities in the composition book, if you have one, and if it has activities on this skill. You also might have created some worksheets with boring or uninteresting beginnings and asked the students to rewrite them so that a reader would want to continue reading.

You might even have hunted down some stories or articles with particularly interesting beginnings and shown them to your students. Your students would be learning about interesting beginnings and you would be teaching, but you would be doing most of the hard work. Worse, students still might not be able to transfer this skill to their own work.

An alternative approach, one that is more effective and much less work for you, depends on students keeping their past compositions in a folder. Using this approach, you simply ask your students to review the introductions to the first three or four compositions they wrote during the year, each selecting the ones with the most interesting and the most boring beginning.

If students cannot find compositions with an interesting beginning, you have the ideal "teachable moment." They can analyze their own work and discuss what makes a good introduction to a composition. You can then require that they rewrite their least effective beginnings so that a reader will want to continue reading.

The difference between the first and second approach is obvious. In the second, your preparation time is used more effectively because the worksheets and examples are already done — by the students. And your students are motivated to work harder editing prose because it is their own.

The second approach also has a cumulative effect. As you introduce new skills, these skills can be applied to past compositions so that, by the end of the school year, students have edited the same compositions for a number of different areas. Imagine the impact of an end-of-year activity that involves selecting the best compositions written during the year that have been carefully edited for many areas and recopied into final form for display or publication.

This end-of-the-year process will provide an exciting opportunity for your students, their parents, and you to see progress.

STRATEGY 9

Encourage students to edit each other's papers before they are handed in.

Another of the Critical Six activities is giving students the opportunity to have their papers reviewed by another student before they have to hand them in. Professional writers are always asking for comments on their work in progress. Train your students to do so as well. Also, the best way to learn how to edit one's own work is by practicing on someone else's.

It will take some practice for your students to learn how to do this in the classroom. The results, however, will be worth the effort. Remember, the more of each other's errors they correct, the fewer for you to correct and the more time for you to enjoy reading and make positive comments on their writing.

It is especially important that students understand exactly what is required when they peer edit — both in terms of behavior and the specific task at hand. You'll probably want to phase it in. Begin by getting students accustomed to reading aloud softly. On a day that they have the first draft of a writing assignment due, ask students to read aloud a paragraph of their own writing in a "one-foot voice" — a voice that cannot be heard by someone standing more than one foot away. If each student reads in a one-foot voice, the noise level in the room should not be disruptive — even if all students are reading at once.

Next, have students select partners. Let them know that if any pair cannot work together for *any* reason you'll regroup them. Give the students a very simple editing task, for example, does your partner's paper have correct manuscript form — date, name, title, margins, whatever your requirements are. Instruct them in how to correct any errors they find and return the papers to their authors for revision into a final draft.

One activity that I used to do to help my students focus on their partner's paper while getting accustomed to working in pairs was to have them choose a title for their partner's paper.

Once your students have practiced peer editing with simple tasks — those I've just suggested, or simple mechanical corrections, for example — and are comfortable and productive working in pairs, you can begin to have them peer edit for more substantive things — interesting beginnings, avoidance of cliches, etc. Always be sure that you've taught the competency and, using the overhead projector, have displayed papers that exhibit the competency and papers that don't before you expect your students to peer edit.

Remember, also, that students are not teachers or professional copy editors. Do not expect that they will be able to make each other's papers perfect. That will never happen because there is no such thing as a perfect paper.

While I'm on the subject, let me say a few more words about managing peer editing. Sometime during the year, have all students switch editing partners. It is necessary to regroup occasionally because partnerships become too easy or too familiar and each student's work needs new critical eyes. Of course you will always selectively regroup partners as any pair fails to accomplish the tasks at hand, either because of lack of understanding (in which case each needs a stronger partner) or too much socializing. As I point out in

Chapter VII, "Finding Time to Teach Writing," the best motivator I've found for keeping students on the assigned task is the prospect of no homework if the work is completed during class time.

One final note about grouping: once you've got a Focus Correction System (Strategy 4) in place, you can group students generally by focus correction areas and have them select editing partners within their focus correction group.

STRATEGY 10

Teach grammar, usage, and mechanics in relationship to the students' current writing problems.

The debate about the place of grammar in a writing program has been the longest and most vociferous of all the controversies surrounding writing instruction. George Hillocks recently researched the question, "What are the most effective ways to teach writing?" He examined 72 carefully selected studies to find trends. Regarding grammar, he states:

> The study of traditional grammar has no effect on raising the quality of student writing and, when overemphasized, can even be deleterious to the development of student writing. Every other focus of instruction had a stronger effect on improving student writing.
>
> School boards, administrators, and teachers who impose the systematic study of traditional school grammar on their students over lengthy periods of time in the name of teaching writing do them a gross disservice, which should not be tolerated. . . . Teachers concerned with teaching standard usage and typographical conventions should teach them in the context of real writing problems" (1983).

Hillocks is not the only one who has questioned the effectiveness of including grammar in the writing curriculum. As early as 1906, Hoyte criticized the study of grammar as an effective tool to improve writing. Studies critical of grammar as a part of the writing curriculum have been a regular section in most books of research on the instruction of writing.

But as any teacher knows, school systems that have a written language arts curriculum inevitably have long and detailed sections on grammar, and major textbook series, which form the backbone of most curricula, prescribe heavy doses of grammar. How can research and practice be so far apart?

A rationale, one that explains much of this discrepancy, lies in the definition of grammar. In an outstanding article on the subject, "Twenty-one Kicks at the Grammar Horse," authors Fraser and Hodson (1978) elaborate on the problem of defining grammar by pointing out just how complex the issue is:

> We must make clear the distinction between **linguistics** and **grammar**. Linguistics is the scientific study of language. Just as in the science of medicine there are particular areas of specialization (radiology, psychiatry, neurology, etc.) so too in linguistics, the linguist may specialize in the study of:
>
> **grammar** (the principles of word and sentence formation)
>
> **rhetoric** (the ways in which writers and speakers organize their "longer forms")
>
> **semantics** (meaning)
>
> **lexicography** (the lexicon or vocabulary — words, their origins, and how they travel and change through time and place)
>
> **usage** (the changing fashions of "correctness" within regional or social dialects)
>
> Grammar, then, is only one of several specialized studies within the general science of linguistics.
>
> Some teachers confuse "grammar" with "grammatical nomenclature" (of whatever school). Grammar is a system of relationships, which is infinitely more than a list of terms, although we do need some terms to be able to talk about the relationships. But equating grammar with the mere lexicon of grammar is like equating science with *The Pelican Dictionary of Science*.

Considering Fraser and Hodson's definitions, now the question becomes *which* grammar should be taught and how?

Clearly, it is a great help to students and teachers alike if everyone knows how to identify nouns, verbs, adjectives, adverbs, prepositions, and pronouns, and understands what a phrase and a clause is. It is very hard to know to avoid run-on sentences without this knowledge. And run-on sentences are one of the most common problems for all writers.

It is also valuable to know usage, what Fraser and Hodson call the "etiquette" of language. Writers and speakers who confuse *between* and *among* or *few* and *less* are able to communicate, but they lose points with literate audiences by committing usage errors that most educated people do not commit.

Students' writing problems will help you decide which grammar you must teach so that you can explain or define their errors as clearly as possible. In general, do not even try to "cover the grammar book." It will take too much time away from actual writing and editing practice. If you teach grammar, teach as little as necessary for your students to be able to speak and write well.

During teacher workshops, I get one question in relationship to grammar that has been very tough to answer. It is usually phrased something like this: "What you say is well and good, and I believe you because I am not sure the grammar I learned helped me improve my writing, but what about the standardized tests my students have to take each spring? These tests are loaded with grammar questions. I will look like an incompetent teacher if my students score poorly on these tests. More importantly, I'll also be doing a disservice to my students who will receive low test scores because they have not been properly prepared."

My response to this question is to ask teachers to take a close look at the test questions to see what test developers are testing for. Many times teachers are surprised to find that they spend 35 percent of their classroom teaching time on grammar that has little direct application to writing and is only represented by a few of the items on a standardized language arts test. Most of the items on standardized language ails tests have questions about usage (to, two, or too; between or among, etc.) or subject-verb agreement, or mechanics. These are best taught using the techniques explained in this book rather than through grammar books or worksheets.

Furthermore, the level of student retention for many extremely abstract grammatical concepts (e.g. the difference between a participial and gerund phrase) is so low that, if these concepts haven't been reviewed immediately before the test, students will score poorly anyway. Remember: to be a good painter you need to know how to mix colors and to experiment to get what you want — but you do not need to know paint chemistry.

STRATEGY 11

Teach editing skills (sentence combining, eliminating unnecessary words and phrases, checking for variety of language, organization, etc.).

Most students want to move from the first draft stage to the copy editing stage without ever moving through the more general editing stage. A very practical way to encourage editing and proofreading lies in the selection of focus correction areas (Strategy 4). The focus areas should be selected to encourage both drafting and editing. See the chart on the following page for examples of focus correction areas that encourage students to focus on the different stages of the writing process.

EXAMPLES OF FOCUS CORRECTION AREAS THAT ENCOURAGE DRAFTING AND REDRAFTING

- Is the topic too general?
- Will the intended audience find the composition interesting?
- Does the composition fulfill the requirements of the assignment?
- Are there sections of the composition that could be eliminated?
- Are there sections that should be expanded?
- Is the composition organized clearly? Would it be easy to summarize?
- Have you written what you most want to say? Does the composition tell the truth?

EXAMPLES OF FOCUS CORRECTION AREAS THAT ENCOURAGE EDITING

- Is the composition easy to read out loud? Does it flow naturally?
- Are the sentences too short? Are they monotonous?
- Is there sentence variety: some long and short sentences, some simple and complex sentences?
- Does the composition have a strong, clear ending?
- Are there cliches or overused words?
- Are there specific details to support general statements?

STRATEGY 12

Teach proofreading skills (punctuation, editing symbols, manuscript form).

Proofreading is the final stage of the writing process. The process begins with topic selection and idea-generating. It then moves to drafting and redrafting for organization and focus. Proofreading includes editing for word choice and sentence structure and, finally, catching mechanical and technical errors. It is at the proofreading stage that it is appropriate to make sure that the i's are dotted and the t's are crossed.

The problem is that most students move from idea-getting to proofreading without passing through the intermediate stages. They are checking for correct end punctuation of a sentence that should not be included in the final draft at all.

It is your ultimate challenge to develop proofreading skills while encouraging students to apply them at the appropriate phase — at the end of the writing process rather than at the very beginning. One of the most effective ways to develop this skill in students is by being a role model (see Strategy 16), demonstrating personally how to take a composition through its many stages, and by providing direct encouragement through one-on-one conferences (Strategy 18) that stress the importance of organization, focus, and experimentation.

I include here a set of basic correction symbols that you can use and reproduce for your students to help in the proofreading process. Note that the symbols have the advantage of including positive comments as well as the more traditional indicators of problem areas. Try to get the faculty in your school to adopt this or a similar set of editing symbols.

When a set of symbols is agreed upon, teachers must teach what the symbol means. Do not assume that because you put *P.* in the margin, students will know you mean "begin a new paragraph." I have seen teachers use *P.* to indicate new paragraph as well as some type of punctuation error or a variety of other problems.

BASIC CORRECTION SYMBOLS

The **Teacher Comment Key** below contains the basic correction symbols. It has an explanatory note at the beginning, so it can be reproduced and distributed to your students. If you are using the Cumulative Writing Folder™ (see page 15) your students will have these symbols right at hand.

Teacher Comment Key

Note to the student: Any time your teacher stars a comment or abbreviation in the margin, it is a signal that it is a positive comment. Look for the starred comments. They will help you find your strengths.

*opening — good beginning for your composition

*closing — good ending for your composition

*w.c. — excellent word choice

*d. — excellent use of detail to support your idea

sp. — the word with a check over it has been misspelled

p. — there's a punctuation error in this line

awk. — this section does not sound right

cap. — there is a capitalization error in this line

frag. — this is a sentence fragment (an incomplete sentence)

run-on — there are two sentences punctuated as one

P. — begin a new paragraph on this line

Give students a copy of a paper that has been corrected using these symbols and ask them to correct the errors. This exercise will help teach them what the symbols mean, and it will help them understand what the editing implications are when the symbols are written on their papers.

You can also choose focus correction areas that encourage proofreading. See Strategy 4 for a more complete list of focus correction areas.

EXAMPLES OF FOCUS CORRECTION AREAS THAT ENCOURAGE PROOFREADING

- Is the penmanship legible?
- Does the writer correctly use quotation marks?
- Does the writer underline the names of books, plays, etc.?
- Are there too many sentences in each paragraph?

Chapter Five

Sharing Activities

STRATEGIES 13 – 18

How often do your students get to share what they've written with anyone but you? Sharing their writing with others provides many benefits:

- If you use the Focus Correction System, having students read each other's first drafts will improve editing skills of both reader and writer.
- Writing for a reader other than the teacher helps students learn how to address different audiences.
- Publishing work and distributing it outside of the classroom or school not only brings positive recognition to the student but to the class (and you) or the school as well.

STRATEGY 13

Provide opportunities for students to read their written work out loud to individuals or to small groups of students.

This last of the Critical Six activities is essential both for sharing and revising written work. One of the conclusions of the National Assessment of Educational Progress is that students do not know how to improve a first draft. This assessment tests the basic skills of students across the country using actual writing samples.

It has found that changes from the first draft to the final draft usually are cosmetic, improving the appearance rather than the quality of the writing. This finding could define the best single statement of the writing problem in our schools: *Students can draft but they can't revise or edit.*

How do we improve students' revision and editing skills? The first, and possibly the most critical, behavior that all teachers must demand is that students read their compositions out loud to themselves. After this step, you should require that student authors hear their compositions read to them by peers (Strategy 9).

Watching a peer struggle with word choice, spelling, or organization may be the single greatest motivator you have to encourage editing. Most students can hear if something is wrong; they can tell where things don't flow or where information is missing.

As I explain in more detail in Strategy 9, you'll need to phase in oral reading. First, require that all students read their compositions out loud to themselves in the "one-foot voice." You will have to remind students to read slowly and carefully, as students have a tendency to rush through their own compositions, reading what they thought they wrote rather than what is actually on the page.

As students become comfortable reading their own work out loud to themselves, require that they read compositions out loud to one other person. When students are comfortable with this step, have them swap papers and have each partner in turn read the paper out loud to the author.

This last step, peer reading paper out loud to author, is the most important, but it usually takes time to get students acclimated to it. My experience has been that it is most helpful to group students by general skill levels — as I suggest in Strategy 4 — and within these groups to let the students select partners.

Occasionally, have students read each other's writing in small groups of four to six. These groups can select the best or the most interesting to be read out loud to the entire class.

Do not have each student read his or her composition to the entire class. This practice can be boring, is time consuming, and is frightening for those who are insecure about their writing or public speaking skills.

In a writing class, the social benefits of reading out loud are as important as the academic benefits. Students learn about others' reactions to their ideas, and they learn about one another. Reading out loud helps create a community of learners, and it is this sense of community that is especially important in a writing class. Also, once students get used to reading out loud, they love it.

STRATEGY 14

Give writing assignments that are meant to be read by readers other than the teacher.

This idea restates one of the recurring themes in this book — the need to create compositions for audiences other than the teacher. In the early grades it is usually less difficult because so many students want to share their work. But as the student becomes older, audiences for compositions usually become more limited.

One very skillful high school teacher overcomes this problem of audience by requiring that students have their writing assignments read by another adult reader who will comment on the work. She takes her system further by providing the adult readers with a simple feedback form they can fill in, with space on the form to explain how they helped improve the composition, if in fact they did provide any assistance.

In addition to instituting systems that require peer editors (see Strategy 9) and other adult readers, teachers can give writing assignments that by their very nature guarantee a wider audience: stories for the school magazine or articles for the school newspaper, reports to the community, and letters are all examples of such assignments.

Daniels and Zemelman in *A Writing Project* list 40 audiences for student writing. Their suggestions range from writing to students in other classrooms and in other schools to asking students to write to chambers of commerce in resort towns or to foreign embassies for information about interesting places or "to the School Board — Report from Room 222. Here's what we're doing. What are you doing?"

STRATEGY 15

Display or "publish" examples of high quality work.

One of the best ways to motivate students is to provide a wide exposure for their compositions. Most students are motivated to polish their writing any time they believe that their compositions will be read by an audience. The larger or more important (e.g., the President) the potential audience, the higher the motivation.

Read out loud the best two or three compositions from each assignment. Ask your students to identify what makes their classmates' writing effective. Keep this list on the bulletin board. As much can be learned from discussing classmates' good writing as from correcting bad writing.

Have bulletin board space for this week's or month's outstanding writers. This idea is especially appropriate for the junior high or high school level, where bulletin boards are rarely used. You will be amazed at how many students will read compositions simply because it is such a novelty to have something on the wall to read.

Issue a classroom literary magazine two to four times a year. Students can select a piece of writing from their folders and polish these works to be included in the magazine. Have volunteers type and make enough copies for grandparents, principals, superintendents, and school committee members. These citizens, who are in a position to defend or criticize schools, see very little of actual student work, especially good writing.

The creative teacher can find a variety of ways to publish, or at least simulate publishing, so that students' work goes beyond the classroom to other students in the school. As an example, here is an assignment for students in grades 5 and above that meets all the criteria for a good assignment and provides an ideal publishing opportunity. Have a second or third grade teacher come into the class with this problem: "Every spring, the students in the second and third grade run out of stories to read. These students are good readers but like to have many choices." The visiting teacher will then ask the students if they could help by writing stories that appeal to second or third graders.

The teacher could describe the types of stories second and third graders like best and the characteristics of a successful story. The teacher could go further by suggesting that she or he will encourage the younger students to write back to the authors telling them what they thought of their stories.

This assignment creates an ideal situation for student writers. They are writing for a known audience, not the teacher, and can select their own topics. As limited a publication as this situation presents, it's greater than many students will ever have.

Students can also collect papers to be put into a book for next year's class. These papers can be arranged by topic or assignment so next year's class can read a few samples of good student compositions. Most students will read straight through such a collection.

Of course, contests are a wonderful source of publication, especially when they are local. Ask your local newspaper to sponsor a contest for a particular grade level. Volunteer to do the preliminary screening so that newspaper staff will only have to read the finalists. Winning compositions then can be published in the paper. In this type of activity there are many winners, including the school system as a whole, because of the positive public relations received from such an event.

STRATEGY 16

Write along with students during class time, on the same writing assignment that they are working on.

This exercise could be considered the ultimate challenge for the writing teacher. The practice of doing your own assignment can create many worthwhile effects, but the most beneficial outcome of doing your own assignments is that it might improve the quality of the writing assignments that you give. And, as Donald Graves is fond of saying, "The teacher shouldn't be the only clothed person in the nudist camp."

I listen to the types of assignments that teachers give and think, "I couldn't write much in response to that topic." The much maligned "What I Did on My Summer Vacation" is mundane but not difficult. It, at least, is based on personal experiences — students can usually make up something.

A second effect of doing your own assignments is that your students see you as a role model; they need to see how difficult it is to plan, write, and refine a composition. I'm convinced that students feel that adults who write just sit down and do it, that the first draft is the final draft, and there is no need to edit. Maybe they feel this way because they only see adults write letters, which are usually the easiest type of writing.

Having students see a teacher grapple with a topic, make false starts, and change and rearrange words is very important. It is the way writing is done: it is hard work, and it requires creativity as well as patience, discipline, and attention to detail.

Writing with the students during class needs to be balanced with the reality of limited teaching time. Some of the best teaching that a writing teacher can do is one-on-one with an individual student while other students are writing and editing.

If you are busy writing your own composition, this opportunity is lost; therefore, you need to balance the need to be a role model, attempting the same assignment as the students, with a need to be available to students when they are writing.

A timesaving compromise is to keep all the drafts of an assignment you wrote with a previous class. Then you do not need to write a new paper each time but can read out loud or share copies with the class to demonstrate the steps you took while working on the assignment.

STRATEGY 17

Write positive comments on students' work.

I often ask teachers to bring a set of recently corrected papers to a workshop. I ask them during the workshop, without looking at the papers, to predict the total number of positive comments on this set of compositions. I then ask teachers to exchange sets and to count the number of positive comments on the set. The actual number of positive comments is *always* significantly lower than each teacher imagines. No one can argue with the value of praise. It's just that we forget to give it.

A best-selling management book, *The One Minute Manager* (Blanchard and Johnson, 1982), describes the typical corporate manager's behavior as "leave alone — zap." Management leaves employees alone until they catch them making a mistake, and then — zap! The authors encourage managers to try to catch their employees doing something right. The same advice applies to writing teachers — try to catch your students doing something right and then tell them what they did that was correct.

You can look inside the cover of any grammar text and find symbols to indicate every imaginable error, but you will not find one symbol for a positive comment! Aside from our habit of trying to indicate every error on every line, it is difficult to say something positive because it takes so much time. Given the number of papers the typical teacher has to correct, writing a positive note on each can lengthen the correcting time to an unbearable amount.

One solution is to use the system indicated in the proof-reading chart in Strategy 12. Using this system, positive comments can be made with a star beside a symbol; for example, *W.C. means excellent word choice. Also, if you use focus correcting as described in Strategy 4, you will have more time per paper to indicate what is right.

As a test of your effectiveness in using positive comments, consider the following assignment. Two times during the year have students write the following three-paragraph essay: In paragraph one ask them to complete the statement, "I need to improve my writing by . . . ." In paragraph two have them finish, "I have improved my writing because . . . ." And in the third paragraph, "One thing I do very well when I write is . . . ." If students cannot think of positive things to say about their writing, help them, and then change the way you are commenting on their papers.

STRATEGY 18

Conduct individual writing conferences with students.

Conducting writing conferences for students can be one of the most rewarding, yet difficult, activities for the teacher. Every teacher realizes how rewarding it is to work with an individual student but also realizes that time is limited. Given the reality of not enough time, the primary purpose of the formal writing conference — as opposed to the fast 10 to 30 second interaction between student and teacher — is to review past work in the student's writing folder (see Strategy 8) and indicate strengths and weaknesses. Together you can select areas for emphasis in the future.

Because lack of time is usually the major problem when implementing individual writing conferences, teachers need to make the most of conference time by using focus correcting to point out strengths as well as weaknesses. Ask the writers what they think they did well and what aspect of the writing needs further work.

Also, use an overhead projector to model this process for your class. Using competent samples, demonstrate how the process works. If you demonstrate and model the process effectively, students can conduct writing conferences with one another.

In his book, *Writing: Teachers and Children at Work*, Graves describes techniques he uses to conduct writing conferences. It is must reading for anyone wanting to fully utilize this strategy. As a key piece of advice, he cautions teachers not to try to do everything with the student in each meeting.

He states, "Teach one thing, no more. The tendency when first working with conferences is to overteach, since the teacher feels that it may be a week before she meets with the child again. Overteaching means the child leaves the conference more confused than when he entered" (1983).

To this point, you have had a chance to assess the status of your writing program using the Writing Program Assessment Survey in Chapter I and have had a chance to review some or all of the 18 strategies discussed in Chapters II through V. The following chapters address questions teachers ask most often: "How do I explain this approach (keeping writing in folders in school, focus correcting, etc.) to parents? How do I find time to teach writing? What skills, or focus correction areas, should I teach? And what other resources do you suggest?"

Chapter Six

Communicating with Parents

Occasionally I am questioned about parents' reactions to two of the Critical Six. If a teacher does Strategy 8 (Provide opportunities for students to review and revise written work completed earlier in the year), students will be keeping compositions in school rather than taking them home, and parents might not see much writing. Also, Strategy 4 (Provide specific information about the criteria you will use to evaluate each assignment) might confuse some parents because they may see papers that have errors that have not been identified.

It has been my experience that parents do not have any problem with these practices as long as they know what is going on. To this end, I have included a copy of a letter you can send to parents that explains these practices very briefly and provides some additional advice and encouragement.

Dear Parent(s):

This year your child will be involved in a writing program that is based on years of research and development and has a few special features.

I will be keeping your child's finished compositions here at school in a writing folder rather than sending them home. The compositions are being kept here so that we can review them to see how writing skills are developing and to look for major problem areas. During the year you are welcome — in fact, I encourage you — to come to school and review and discuss the compositions.

Another major feature of this program is called focus correcting. The focus correcting system is based on the belief that student writing improves more quickly when the student works to improve a few writing problems at a time. It will be hard for me not to correct every error on every paper, but this year I will be indicating errors on each paper in only one, two, or three areas. These areas will be announced in advance so that my students can focus their energies on them. We will keep a record of all the focus correction areas we cover during the year.

Parents often ask, "How can I help?" Let me make a few suggestions. *Be a helper and an encourager, not a critic.* Provide a quiet place to write with good lighting and a dictionary. Talk about the assignments and help your son or daughter get lots of ideas. Look for good things in the composition. And, if you are asked to review a composition, read the composition out loud. Ask if it sounds right. You'll be surprised at how many of their own mistakes they will be able to hear.

If you have any questions or comments about this program or about anything else we are doing, please call.

Sincerely,

Chapter Seven

Finding Time to Teach Writing

The goal of this chapter is to present a master plan or schedule to help make teaching writing easier. This plan is based on the following assumptions:

- Any **basic** writing plan should not require an unreasonable amount of teacher preparation time — no more than one to two hours per week on the average.

- Any **basic** writing plan should not require an unreasonable amount of classroom time — not more than one third of all the time available to teach language arts. Let's assume that the typical classroom period is 45 minutes and that there are 20 teaching days in a month. One-third of this time equals 300 minutes or five hours a month for language arts. If there is more time, great, but I have found very few teachers who feel they have even this much time.

- Any **basic** writing plan should produce a reasonable quantity of compositions during the school year — nine or ten compositions per semester or one composition every other week.

I've devised a system that meets these criteria. It should not require more than one hour per week preparation time; it takes approximately 320 minutes, or five hours per month, to carry out; and it results in a minimum of 20 final drafts per year. (In fact, if you select one of the alternative approaches, students will produce 30 final drafts per year. More on that later.)

GETTING THE SYSTEM IN PLACE

Before you actually begin using this system, you need to review writing samples to diagnose two to four of your classes' most serious writing problems. To make this task easier, ask yourself this question: "If I could eliminate or substantially reduce only four or five writing problems, what would they be?" Be careful: consider more than the "big three" — Capitalization, Spelling, and Punctuation. Consider other areas as well: Are the papers too long or too short? Does the writer try to capture the reader's interest in the first sentence or paragraph? Does the writer use specific details to support general statements? Are the sentences too long and confusing? (See Chapter VIII, "What Writing Skills Should Be Taught," for additional information.)

Write down the two, three, or four most serious writing problems. Your instructional goal this year will be to correct these problems. If you find you are making great strides in these areas, you can always add one or two more, but be aware that the most common problem in writing instruction is that teachers try to do too much in too short a time and inevitably end up having little long-term impact.

THE COLLINS SYSTEM
A Monthly Plan

Week Number One

Three times this week, on Monday, Wednesday, and Friday, teach a 20-minute lesson to the total class on how to improve one of the problems you listed as critical. For example, if you have selected run-on sentences, on Monday teach lessons on subjects and verbs or on compound sentences. You might want to begin with a pretest that requires your students to identify run-ons and correct them.

On Wednesday give your students a lesson on how to correct run-ons or opportunities to practice; and on Friday give a short posttest to see the effect of your instruction, or ask your students to select a specific composition from their writing folders and edit for run-on sentences. You might need to provide additional practice in the future for those students who still cannot correct a run-on sentence. Total time for week one: approximately 60 minutes (3 x 20).

Week Number Two

Monday: Announce a composition topic in a general way. Let students know that the final draft will be due Friday morning, at the start of class. Also let students know that a first draft is due on Thursday. Encourage students to ask questions to clarify the assignment or to add new approaches to the assignment that might make it more interesting or exciting. Total time: 15 minutes.

Tuesday: Brainstorm ideas about the assignment with the students. Fill the air with ideas and answer any questions about the specifics of the assignment. Total time: 15 minutes.

Wednesday: Spend 20 minutes teaching a lesson on run-on sentences to those students who did not pass the post-test last Friday. Give those students who did pass the post-test an opportunity to begin composing their first drafts. For all students, a first draft is due Thursday at the beginning of class. Total time: 20 minutes.

Thursday: Peer editors read the compositions out loud in pairs and check to see if the author followed the assignment and if the composition is easy to read. Students work together editing the first draft for the focus correction area, in this case, run-on sentences. When this aspect is completed, students can begin recopying their papers into a final draft. Students who are finished may hand in finished compositions; those who need more time must take their compositions home to complete. Total time: 45 minutes. (Note: You should be available during this time to discuss student problems and answer questions.)

From my experience, the best way to group for peer editing is in ability-grouped teams of two. You might find that some students are not able to work with other students without being very disruptive. These students are best placed close to your desk so that you can monitor behavior. But, because the time limits are tight, students tend to work very hard to help one another and to get the compositions recopied so that they do not have homework.

Friday: At the beginning of the day, students must hand in compositions that were not completed on Thursday. This deadline discourages students from trying to copy compositions during other subjects. I also like having the opportunity to talk with students before school to discuss their reaction to the assignment, writing problems, etc. The total time for week two: 95 minutes.

Week Number Three

Monday: Hand back corrected compositions. *These compositions should have been very easy to correct because you were focus correcting, that is, correcting them only for the major problem area that was introduced during Week One.* Take about ten minutes to discuss how the class did and read some of the better papers out loud so that students have a sense of what you consider a good composition. Repeat Week Two's schedule by introducing a new topic. Total time for week three: 105 minutes.

Week Number Four

Monday: Hand back corrected compositions. Again, these compositions should have been easy to correct because you were focus correcting. Discuss how the class did and read some of the better papers out loud so that students have a sense of what you consider a good composition. For the rest of the week you can select from three options:

Option 1: If most or all of your students are having difficulties improving their compositions in the area that you have been focusing on, repeat Week One (three sessions for 20 minutes) with 60 minutes of instruction in the problem area. Total time Option 1: 60 minutes.

Option 2: If only 30-60 percent of the students are having problems with the focus area, work with this group following the agenda for Week One and give the remaining students opportunities for independent writing. The independent writers will have 60 minutes available during the week to write a second composition. The students who are having trouble with the focus correction area will receive direct instruction from you in that area and will be tested on Friday to demonstrate mastery of that area. The test and the composition will count equally for students' grades at the end of the term. Total time Option 2: 60 minutes.

Option 3: A third approach is to spend 20 minutes teaching how to eliminate problems in the focus area on Monday and then, on Thursday and Friday, give students the opportunity to review compositions that they have kept in a folder and select the one that they think is best. Ask the students to review this composition with a peer editor and to improve it in every possible way.

This third draft will essentially be "published," that is, included in a classroom literary magazine or local newspaper, displayed during parents night, displayed on the walls of the classroom, sent to the principal, or any other way that comes to mind. Total time for Option 3: 80 minutes.

Other Considerations

To use this system the teacher has to keep student compositions in school in a folder because students need to be able to review earlier compositions. As the year goes on and new focus correction areas are added, students can use compositions that were written earlier in the year to practice editing skills. Also, students should be permitted to select their own topics from time to time.

Do not always have mechanical errors as focus correction areas. Try to mix focus correction areas — areas that are stylistic (e.g., a beginning that makes the reader want to read on) with areas that are mechanical (e.g., using correct end marks). *If you always focus on just mechanical errors, students will eventually equate writing with avoiding mechanical errors rather than as communicating with others.*

Remember, the first month using this system will be the hardest and will take more time. After the system is in place for a month or two, expect it to go more smoothly and expect the students to appreciate being able to predict the work load in advance.

MASTER PLAN

	Monday	Tuesday
Week one	Intensive instruction to eliminate problem in major focus correction area. **20 minutes**	
Week two	Announce and discuss composition assignment. **15 minutes**	Brainstorm ideas about the assignment. **20 minutes**
Week three	Hand back corrected compositions from previous week. Read a few of the best.	
Week four	Hand back corrected/compositions from previous week. Read a few of the best. Select Options A, B, or C. For example, Option C: Lesson on skills to eliminate errors in the focus correction area. **20 minutes**	

Wednesday	Thursday	Friday
Intensive instruction to eliminate problem in major focus correction area. **20 minutes**		Intensive instruction to eliminate problem in major focus correction area. **20 minutes**
Lesson on skills to eliminate errors in the focus correction area. **20 minutes**	Students work in teams to read compositions out loud and peer edit for focus correction area. **45 minutes**	Final draft of composition due today.
←—REPEAT WEEK TWO————————————————————————————→		
	Select best composition from folder. Review with peer editor. Improve it every possible way. Recopy. **30 minutes**	**30 minutes**

Chapter Eight

What Writing Skills Should Be Taught

DETERMINING FOCUS CORRECTION AREAS

After teachers find out about focus correcting, one of the questions they most frequently ask is, "Do you have a list of focus correction areas by grade level?" For years I have been working on an answer to this question, and I finally have one in which I have confidence: *no!* After searching through research reports, curriculum guides, and theoretical papers on composition skills, I have not found a research-based description of writing skills by grade level with which I am comfortable. Therefore, in response to this question, I have developed a hierarchy of competencies and related focus correction areas that, while not grade related, represent a continuum of writing skill levels. These levels have been classroom tested in urban and suburban schools at many different grade levels. The five competency levels and the focus correction areas for each one are described at the end of this chapter.

I recommend that the levels be used in the following way. First, take a writing sample of final drafts from students and group the sample compositions into three piles: the best samples, average samples, and poorest samples. Another way of thinking of this grouping is to create a pile of samples that would have received a grade of A, a second pile that would have received grades of B or C, and a third pile that would have received grades of D or F. Second, read over each pile of papers carefully. Third, match each pile with one of the Writing Competency Levels, I-V, described in the following pages.

For example, if you find the papers with the poorest writing fulfill all the needs listed in Level I, consider their authors to have attained Level II status and use the focus correction areas listed in Level II for this group. Your middle group may meet all the needs listed for Level II and need the skills for Level III, while your top group might demonstrate the competencies for Level IV. You can help this group develop the skills for Level V. To further determine if you have placed students in the correct group, you may wish to give each group assignments designed to demonstrate the competencies of the Level you feel they have achieved.

Consider the focus correction areas listed under each competency as suggestions. For example, if your students seem to be competent Level II writers with the exception of one of the focus correction areas, add that area to Level III and place your students in Level III. Likewise, if your students need most of the skills listed in Level IV but are competent in one or two, replace these with other skills they lack. Let the level serve as a guide and a format for organizing your program.

Consider doing most of your large group instruction to the middle group (probably 60-70 percent of all students), and provide small group instruction for the bottom and the top groups. The bottom group (probably 10-15 percent of total) should receive most of your individual attention, while the top group (probably 10-15 percent) should get the least amount of attention. Because the top group has good basic skills and presumably high motivation, the assignment and a short explanation of a focus correction area, together with your editing, should be sufficient to help these students improve.

Each competency level described below includes the following characteristics: an indication of a minimum composition length; a required style (narration, description, exposition), and suggested focus correction areas. The lists of focus correction areas are short because the skills that are listed are difficult, and the list assumes that students will have *mastered* the skills, that is, can consistently apply the skills in their writing. Remember, the main problem of good writing teachers is the irrational yet powerful fear that "If I don't cover it, no one else will." Do not try to teach too many skills.

WRITING COMPETENCIES FOR LEVEL I

To be competent Level I writers, students will produce five related sentences that tell a story. The composition should be *understandable* and should demonstrate competencies in the following focus correction areas:

1. Legible handwriting.
2. Use of complete sentences.
3. Correct capitalization at the beginning of sentences and correct capitalization of proper nouns.
4. Correct end punctuation.

WRITING COMPETENCIES FOR LEVEL II

To be competent Level II writers, students will produce five related sentences that are *easily understood* in *two* separate writing samples: One should require students to tell a story and one should require students to describe a place or a thing. The two writing samples will demonstrate competencies in the following focus correction areas:

1. Sentences developed to include descriptive language, that is, use of adjectives and adverbs.
2. Use of sensory, concrete vocabulary.
3. Avoidance of the overuse of *so, and,* and *then.*
4. Subject-verb agreement.
5. All competencies listed for previous levels.

WRITING COMPETENCIES FOR LEVEL III

To be competent Level III writers, students should produce five to fifteen related sentences that should be *easily understood* in *two* separate writing samples: One sample should require students to tell a story, and one sample should require students to describe a place or thing. The two writing samples should demonstrate competencies in the following focus correction areas:

1. A first sentence or introduction that makes the reader want to continue reading.
2. Use of varied sentence lengths and use of varied sentence beginnings (introductory prepositional phrase, introductory adverbial phrase, etc.).
3. All competencies listed for previous levels.

WRITING COMPETENCIES FOR LEVEL IV

To be competent Level IV writers, students will produce *three* multi-paragraph writing samples that are *easily understood.* One sample should require students to tell a story, a second should require students to describe a place or a thing, and a third sample should require students to support an opinion or explain a position. The three writing samples should demonstrate competencies in the following focus correction areas:

1. Use of varied sentence patterns, that is, some sentences that are simple, some compound, and some complex.
2. Correct internal punctuation, that is, correct use of commas, quotation marks, and semicolons.
3. Use of specific details to support general statements.
4. All competencies listed for previous levels.

WRITING COMPETENCIES FOR LEVEL V

To be competent Level V writers, students will produce *three* multi-paragraph writing samples that are *easily understood.* One sample should require students to tell a story, a second should require students to describe a place or a thing, and a third sample should require students to state an opinion or explain a position. These samples should demonstrate competencies in the following focus correction areas:

1. An opening paragraph that introduces the topic.
2. A concluding paragraph or statement that sums up the topic.
3. Use of transitions between paragraphs.
4. Concise writing — not wordy.
5. All competencies listed for previous levels.

Beyond Level V, it's up to you. Look at the lists of 24 focus correction areas provided in Chapter III, Strategy 4, or generate new areas based on the assignments you are giving. If you are teaching the research paper, you could make up a list of 30 or 40 focus correction areas; and this list would be very different from a list of focus correction areas for a short story or a business letter.

As you make new levels, *remember not to select focus correction areas that just focus on mechanical errors* (e.g., spelling or punctuation). Doing so will kill your writing program because students will write to avoid errors rather than to communicate.

Chapter Nine

Final Thoughts

This book was written to provide a brief, straightforward guide for teachers who want to teach writing effectively. I've provided the Writing Program Assessment Survey (Chapter I) so that teachers can determine the effectiveness of their current program. I then detailed 18 specific strategies (Chapters II-V) and a plan to pull these strategies into a coherent whole (Chapters VII and VIII). This approach is practical — all the ideas have been tested in classrooms throughout the United States — and effective — the reports from schools that have implemented these ideas are glowing.

But in my attempt to be practical, I may have put the accent on the wrong syllable. I may have emphasized the form (classroom management and teaching techniques) over the content (the quality of student ideas), and in doing so violated one of my own favorite focus correction areas — developing ideas in relationship to their importance. If there is one commandment in writing, it is this: writing can only be as good as the content. Good content can carry weak form. Good form can't carry weak content.

But how to get good content? This is a particularly difficult question, especially because one person's idea about the quality of another's ideas is very subjective. In fact I've always tried to discourage teachers from using a two-grade marking system, one for content and one for mechanics, because of the subjectivity involved and because of the amount of time it takes to sort out the metaphysical difference between a "C+" and a "B−" idea. Don't use grades or the fear of grades as motivation to develop good content.

To get good content, spend your time where it will do the most good: Provide opportunities for students to discuss the assignment (Strategy 1) and provide opportunities for students to get more information about the assignment (Strategy 2). Talk and time are related to the quality of ideas. Giving students an opportunity for large and small group discussion and time to think and to let their subconscious work on the problem or an idea is the best approach.

In the one-month plan described in Chapter VII, the writing is assigned on Monday, but the first draft is not due until Thursday and the final draft, until Friday. The time schedule suggested provides students the opportunity to think and discuss and to get more information about the topic. This cannot happen if an assignment is given on a Monday and expected on Tuesday.

Be patient. Some of the suggestions in this book appear to be simple management techniques and they are, but they can create major changes in the climate of your classroom. Focus correcting takes getting used to by both teachers and students. For students who are not accustomed to helping one another or for teachers who are uncomfortable with group work, peer editing might take months to establish as a smoothly running process.

Even a technique as simple as oral reading takes time to establish — students almost always read too fast and too loudly at the beginning. But the changes are worth the time and effort.

In an urban middle school that I recently worked with, I stressed just these three techniques — focus correcting, peer editing, and oral reading — and in one year the school went from last place (24 out of 24) to first in the district's writing assessment. These techniques have powerful effects!

Share these techniques with other teachers. Most students experience a different writing program with every teacher they have. One year the writing program is journal and narrative writing and the next, it is grammar and the research paper. The standards, the teaching techniques, and the skills taught vary so widely that there is no opportunity for mastery or refinement of skills over time. Encourage other teachers to use the techniques that make up the Critical Six. Let these techniques become the basis for your school or school district writing program. No teacher can do it all in a year. You need to get other teachers to reinforce the same behaviors. You'll be amazed at the results.

Chapter Ten

Further Reading

The *Effective Writing Teacher* will help you create or refine your current writing program, but it will not answer all of your questions. Listed below are resources that will extend the ideas presented in this book.

Books on how to write: You can't teach what you don't know; therefore all writing teachers should be familiar with a few of the classics on writing. Two of the undisputed classics are *The Elements of Style* by William Strunk and E.B. White (Macmillan, 1979) and *On Writing Well* by William Zinsser (Harper and Row, 1976). Both are short, clear, and easy-to-read and serve as models for what they preach.

A new contender for future "classic" status is James Kilpatrick's *The Writer's Art* (Andrews, McMeel & Parker, 1984). Kilpatrick's book is my favorite of the three only because it's longer and covers more ground. In his chapter "Faith, Hope, and Clarity" he states, "I have a theory about writing. The theory goes to this effect: the chief difference between good writing and better writing may be measured by the number of imperceptible hesitations the reader experiences as he goes along." Three cheers for reading out loud! His chapter on "The Things We Ought Not to Do" and "The Things We Ought to be Doing" could provide the basic set of skills for any high school writing curriculum.

Books on designing writing programs: My major concern (and I hope it is apparent by now) is that schools have good writing programs as well as good writing teachers. In the area of designing writing programs, three books stand out: *The Handbook for Planning an Effective Writing Program — Kindergarten Through Grade 12* (Publication sales: California State Department of Education, P.O. Box 271, Sacramento, CA 85802), is a 72-page handbook with an excellent review of the research in writing, a comprehensive checklist that can be used to evaluate a school's writing program, and an excellent description of the writing process, complete with suggested activities and references.

Teaching Writing: Problems and Solutions by Shirley Boes Neill (American Association of School Administrators, 1801 North Moore Street, Arlington, VA 22209) is loaded with information; it contains interviews with Donald Graves and Donald Murray, case studies describing excellent writing programs in schools across the nation, and chapters on inservice training, the principal's role in promoting good writing, and evaluation.

Writing in the Schools: Improvement Through Effective Leadership by Allan Glatthorn (National Association of Secondary School Principals, 1904 Association Drive, Reston, VA 22091) focuses on improving writing at the secondary school level but is of value to any administrator trying to design a program. Glatthorn's book is filled with survey forms and checklists that will help involve staff in program design while raising their awareness of the issues involved. He has excellent short chapters on working with parents and supervising the writing program.

Books on teaching writing: Begin with the classics. Peter Elbow's *Writing With Power* (Oxford University Press, 1981), Donald Murray's *A Writer Teaches Writing* (Houghton Mifflin, 1968), and Donald Grave's *Writing: Teachers and Children at Work* (Heinemann, 1983). All three are excellent, but if I had to select one, I would pick *Writing: Teachers and Children at Work*. This book is divided into five sections: Start to Teach Writing, Make the Writing Conference Work, Help Children Learn the Skills They Need, Understand How Children Develop as Writers, and Document Children's Writing Development. It is a must for primary and elementary school teachers, but it does not address, or pretend to, the unique problems of a junior high or high school teacher who must see 100+ students each day in sharply defined blocks of time.

High school teachers will want to check out Arthur Applebee's *Writing in the Secondary School* (National Council of Teachers of English, 1981) for its descriptions of how writing is being taught in secondary schools and its recommendations about what should be happening. Applebee does not talk directly about how to teach writing but his descriptions of excellent classrooms can serve as models for the enterprising teacher.

The National Council of Teachers of English Catalog lists and describes hundreds of interesting works, from books and papers to cassettes and literary maps. The section on writing is excellent and many of the books it suggests can be purchased through the catalog. The catalog can be obtained by writing to the National Council of Teachers of English, 1111 Kenyon Road, Urbana, IL 61801.

Two other works every teacher should have include Roger McCaig's *A Model for the Evaluation of Student Writing* (Grosse Pointe Public Schools, 389 St. Clair Avenue, Grosse Pointe, MI 48230, which describes a model for evaluating compositions from grades 1 to 10. It is especially helpful because it provides more than 60 pieces of actual student writing arranged by grade level from worst to best. Teachers can look at what is considered average or good writing at their grade level and get a sense of how their students compare. The other must is an article — "Twenty-one Kicks at the Grammar Horse," by Ian S. Fraser and Lynda M. Hodson, in the *English Journal*, December, 1978. Fraser and Hodson answer the most commonly asked questions about grammar with style and grace. They define what grammar is, why it should be taught, and how it should be taught. You'll probably want to quote them.

References

Applebee, Arthur. *Writing in the Secondary School: English and the Content Areas.* NCTE Research Report No. 21. National Council of Teachers of English, Urbana, Illinois, 1981.

Blanchard, Kenneth and Spencer Johnson. *The One Minute Manager.* Morrow and Company, Inc., New York, 1982.

Daniels, Harvey and Steven Zemelman. *A Writing Project.* Heinemann Educational Books, Exeter, New Hampshire, 1985.

Fraser, Ian and Lynda Hodson. "Twenty-one Kicks at the Grammar Horse." *English Journal*, December, 1978.

Graves, Donald H. *Writing: Teachers and Children at Work.* Heinemann Educational Books, Exeter, New Hampshire, 1983.

Hillocks, George. *What Works in Teaching Composition: A Media-Analysis of Experimental Treatment Studies* (memo). University of Chicago, Chicago, Illinois, 1984.

National Assessment of Educational Progress. *Write/Rewrite: An Assessment of Revision Skills.* Writing Report No. 05-W-04, 1977. Available from Superintendent of Documents, U.S. Government Printing Office, Washington, D.C. 20402.

Smith, Frank. "Myths of Writing." *Language Arts*, Volume 58, No. 7, October, 1981.